OUTDOOR PLACES

BY JEFFREY WEISS

Photography by Jon Elliott

Additional photography by David Leach, Michael Kanouff, Yolande Flesch, Yudit Flesch, Nancy McCord, and Jeffrey Weiss

W · W · NORTON & COMPANY
New York   London

Copyright © 1980 by Jeffrey Weiss

Published simultaneously in Canada by George J. McLeod Limited,

Toronto. Printed in the United States of America.

All Rights Reserved

First Edition

Library of Congress Cataloging in Publication Data

Weiss, Jeffrey.
    Outdoor places.

    1. Landscape gardening—United States—Pictorial works. 2. Gardens—United States—Pictorial works. 3. Landscape architecture—United States—Pictorial works. 4. Decks (Architecture, Domestic)—United States—Pictorial works. 5. Patios—United States—Pictorial works. 6. Balconies—United States—Pictorial works. 7. Outdoor furniture—United States—Pictorial works. 8. Vernacular architecture—United States—Pictorial works. I. Title.
SB473.F84   1980   712'.6   80–13090
ISBN 0–393–01365–0
ISBN 0–393–00976–9 (pbk.)

1 2 3 4 5 6 7 8 9 0

GARDEN. The very word summons a vision of serenity and peace, and, indeed, throughout civilization, gardens, and their modern miniatures, balconies, terraces, rooftops, and patios, have provided us with a double pleasure—the comfort, safety, and privacy of our own homes and the joys of nature.

Hot and dusty countries gave us the cool oasis with its sparkling pool and shade trees; in cooler climates, a warm and sunny spot shielded from the wind provided the perfect outdoor retreat. The walled gardens of medieval days allowed royal ladies to take the air secure from the woes and gaze of the outer world. In wilderness areas, the garden always provided a certain "taming" of natural elements, protection from a hostile environment.

Our wilderness is different. It is "civilization" that threatens and encroaches upon us from all sides. Cities are larger, suburbs sprawl ever wider; the country is more distant. More and more we feel the need to bring nature back closer to us. As city parks grow more crowded, and even dangerous, we seek a little park of our own, a private outdoor place.

The small-garden movement is not regional. Pictured here are gardens in Little Rock and Washington and Berkeley, in New Orleans and Woodstock and New York City, in Showerhouse, Colorado, and Memphis, Tennessee.

Garden building is taking its place beside other building arts, as an extension of the house itself. People are choosing outdoor furniture, designing rock gardens, displays, pools, and fountains, and laying down patio floors and decks, with the same care and creativity they employ in their dining and living rooms. *Outdoor Places* is not a practical guide to garden landscaping. But, as I hoped to show people what they could achieve for themselves in *Made with Oak, Lofts,* and *Rugs,* so once again I hope to inspire those interested in improving their own garden plots—or just to delight with the beautiful possibilities of outdoor living. *Outdoor Places* shows how people with ingenuity, creativity, and some means have turned their outdoor spaces into truly beautiful living places.

Jeffrey Weiss

2

3

4

6

7

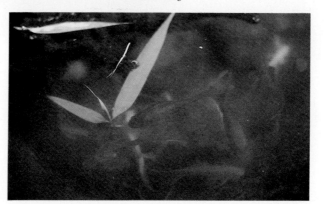

8

10

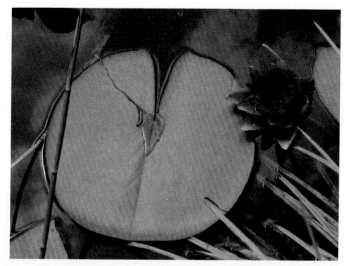

11

12

13

16

17

18

19

20

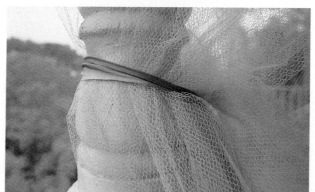

21

22

23

24

25

26

27

28

29

32

33

34

35

36

37

38

39

40

41

42

43

44

45

46

48

49

50

51

52

53

55

56

57

59

60

61

62

63

64

65

66

67

68

69

70

71

72

73

74

75

76

79

80

81

82

83

85

86

87

88

89

90

91

92

93

94

96

97

98

99

100

102

103

104

105

106

107

108

110

111

112

116

117

118

120

121

122

125

126

127

129

130

131

132

133

134

136

137

140

141

142

143

144

145

146

147

148

149

150

151

152

153

154

155

156

157

158

159

160

161

162

163

164

165

166

167

168

169

170

172

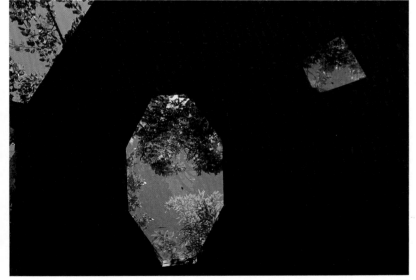

171

173

174

175

177

178

179

180

182

183

184

185

186

187

188

189

190

191

192

193

194

195

196

197

198

204

205

206

207

PHOTO CREDITS